Sister's are like Cookies & Milk

Whether things
are sweet or crummy,
they're better together.

Inspired
by Faith

Sisters are like Cookies & Milk
©Product Concept Mfg., Inc.

Sisters Are Like Cookies & Milk
ISBN 978-0-9835438-2-4

Published by Product Concept Mfg., Inc.
2175 N. Academy Circle #200, Colorado Springs, CO 80909

©2011 Product Concept Mfg., Inc. All rights reserved.

All scripture quotations are from the King James version
of the Bible unless otherwise noted.

Written and Compiled by Sharon Valleau
in association with Product Concept Mfg., Inc.

Sisters
are like
Cookies
& Milk

A sister is a little bit of childhood
that can never be lost.

Being Sisters...

It's Not for Sissies!

Sisters... those people who you could disown one minute and passionately defend the next. They know where you come from and understand why you are the way you are.

They know the gifts you showed at an early age, and they'll remind you of them if you ever lose your way. Sisters cheer for you and jeer at you and marvel as they witness your becoming.

A lifetime of sparring with them sharpens your wit and toughens your skin just a little bit.

Prayers for our Sisters

Dear God,
My sister and I are old now, but
when I look at her, I still see the
round faced little girl who shared
double Popsicles with me, kept
my secrets, and spent hours of
days of a life just hanging out
with me, enjoying being…related.

Dear God,
About my sister…
I guess I'll keep her.

Dear God,

My dear sister gets on my last best nerve!
You know the one that I reserve for company?

She's so frustrating! She doesn't do things
the way I do, and can you believe the things
she says sometimes? She doesn't do anything
I tell her to do, and we can hardly spend any
time together without a little friction.

But Lord, I still have her here! I can see her
face and hear her voice, her laugh.
Thank you, God!
Please leave her right here on my nerve.

(I think it's right beside my heart.)

Dear God,

Do I get points for all of the times that
I resisted the urge to tell my sister off
when she was taking such pleasure
in making me mad?

Dear God,
Is it okay if I don't give my
sister power of attorney
over my living will?

Dear God,
When we were younger, it was
really cool that I got all of the
cute boyfriends and was the
popular sister. Funny – none of
that matters now. Little kids
don't know how time changes
the definition of a good life.

Dear God,
Were you watching when my sister
and I made fun of people in church?
I mean I'm sure you were watching,
but surely some of those sermons
bored you, too.

Dear God,

Thank you for forgiving me for wishing my sister any bad fortune.

Forgive me for feeling jealous towards my sister for her success and money and position...and her wonderful husband and her great car and her remodeling... and her surgeries to reverse aging, and her frequent flyer miles from all of the places she's visited around the world, and...

Lord, you know I love her, and if she didn't have those things, I would be praying all of those blessings for her. Hmmm...I never thought about it like that!

Thank you, God! Our little talks always help.

Amen.

Speaking
of my
Sister...

A girl daydreams of wealth and fame,
eternal youth, some handsome men.
A woman sometimes wishes
she could just laugh like she's five again.
Come on, Sis! Remember when?

Sisterhood is a lifetime
of competing emotions:
I love her! I can't stand her!
I love her! I can't stand her!

Sisters should have emotional debit accounts. If you withdraw too much support, you have to give back 'till you're out of the red. You can't go crying to your sister until you top off your balance by listening to her troubles a little bit.

Even though with the way Mom liked her best, she probably has no troubles. Oops, there go ten credits!

My sister is so competitive
she pouts when she loses at solitaire.

If you only could have seen what my sister did to a fashion doll, you would know never to mess with her!

I'm not saying my sister's mean,
but if I were you,
I'd hide my broom when she's around.

Some people see
the glass as half full...
my sister thinks the glass is
just there to distort her figure
and make her feel fat.

My sister claims I can be rude, self-centered, judgmental, impatient, and a little catty. I'll admit it – sometimes she's right, but she has to admit that I can get away with it because of my irresistible charm. Yep, it's like hiding medicine in a candy shell.

When you've really gotten on the wrong track, you can depend on your sister to be honest. Especially when she's telling Mom all about it.

They should write a book about
me and my sister.
   "Eat. Criticize. Nitpick."
I wonder who'll star in the movie?

My sister should have a 24-hour
radio station and an FCC license
just to air her grievances. It could
be called WYME. It would need to
be up near the end of the dial to
cover all her mega-hurtz.

For some reason, when reality-TV
contestants get in a screaming, hair-
pulling, knock-down-drag-out, I get
all misty-eyed and think of you, Sis.

My sister can make a mean sandwich.
She can also play a mean game of Canasta.
As well as play a mean piano concerto.
There's a pattern here, if you know what
I mean.

My sister – cheap?

Why, just because she
was born with a plastic
spoon in her mouth…

In our memories, my sister and I had the
perfect girlie bedroom in a neat, bright
cottage, with a picket fence, sunshine and
flowers.

Of course, we've blocked out all memory
of smelly socks, dust bunnies under the
bed, piles of clothes everywhere, and
"experiments" growing on the windowsill…

Speaking of my Sister...

My sister and I took a scuba diving class and they told us to find a "buddy." So of course, I got as far away from my sister as I could. Just kidding. I trust her to watch my ever-so-much-more-shapely back. And the best thing is, under water she can't run her mouth.

DNA research is causing all kinds of plants and animals to be re-classified. For example, the banana aphid was found not to be related to the ginger aphid. This is all rival siblings need — an excuse to "reclassify" their relatives!

The last thing I'd ever do is embarrass my sister...
There are many other little irritations I'd employ first.

Sisters are like credit cards – it's great to have one in a pinch, but you get into trouble when you try to use them to get everything you want!

When we were kids, my sister and I played "Astronaut," "Race Car Driver," and "Engineer." It wasn't that we didn't play "girly" games, too, but I guess we were ahead of our time.

(And no one told us those things were for boys.)

Twenty percent of Americans are only-children. They'll never know the delights of running to tattle, teasing and pranking, up-ending the game board when they're losing, or just hanging out quietly doing nothing with someone else who you're totally comfortable with. Pity.

My sister was so bossy that she signed her greeting cards like performance reviews:

"Happy Birthday, Mom. I appreciate your effort this year. Please continue to be good to me."

It did little good to point out to my sister that the world didn't revolve around her. As far as she was concerned, that was delusional thinking from someone of obvious lesser intelligence.

My sister was mad at me for a whole semester in junior high. Just because I started a small but completely innocuous rumor that she had to use men's heavy-duty odor-absorbing foot powder by the case. Talk about sensitive!

I never had to worry about breaking bad news to my parents and seeing the disappointment on their faces. My sister always did it for me!

Having a sister teaches invaluable
negotiation skills that usually
began with "if you don't tell on me,
I won't tell on you."

Don't believe in spontaneous
human combustion?
Try telling your sister her new
$200 hairdo looks cheap.

When my sister visited my crummy apartment, I told her I was into minimalism. Actually, it was a case of minimal money. I said it with a snooty air though. I hope she bought it.

Never take your sister on a trip to Europe. Not if she's cuter than you and there's any chance of meeting a nice dashing count. The only thing dashing will be your hopes. Don't ask me how I know.

My older sister's first job was at a burger joint. She came home smelling of onions and talking of boys – a heady mixture of independence and fun. I blame my addiction to burgers on that.

"Tell me you're NOT dating a glorified checkout clerk," my sister said. Twenty years later that "glorified checkout clerk" and I are going on a world cruise. I won't tell her about the fabulous food, my new resort wardrobe, our top-deck cabin… but I will keep praying for humility.

True sisterhood is being happy for your sister even when her engagement ring is two times sparklier. Of course, it probably has a flaw. You know it does.

I'll always keep the door to communication open with my sister, no matter what. Someday we'll be 40, then 50…and (keep going) 60, 70, 80, and we'll be over our stuff and need a friend!

Who else but a sister would tell you your new, expensive perfume smells like fresh grass clippings?

There's this Mexican dance where two people face each other, trade repartee and stamp the floor. Who knew? My sister and I could have taken our show on the road.

When my life took a bad turn, I didn't really try to hide it from my sister. I think I secretly hoped she'd sit me down and try to talk some sense into me, in her blunt way. Because her blunt way is 1000 times softer than the stuff life throws at you if you stay off track too long.

You know what I love about sisters? You don't have to explain why you're so neurotic, insecure, risk-averse and self-conscious. You know what I hate about sisters? You can't get away with reinventing your backstory.

My sister likes to peer at my house-plants with this pained look on her face. She doesn't know this, but I gave her power of attorney over them in my will. Then she can tsk-tsk about my aphids to her heart's content!

My sister got anti-aging injections and can't make her pinched, disapproving expression anymore. I know! I ate a whole bag of onion rings just to watch her try.

My sister is adopted, but she's every bit
my "real" sister. We fight, slam doors,
smart off and roll our eyes just like
bio sisters! Yeah, and we protect each
other and feel better just being together
without talking, we cheer for each other.
And our hearts break for each other.
That's real love.

I dearly love my sister!
She always way overestimates
my intelligence...
and underestimates
my waistline.

Don't take a friend with you
swimsuit-shopping. Take your
sister. It'll be painful, but that's
one time you need the cold,
hard truth. One of many.

We're sisters…
held together by family ties,
favorite memories,
and lots and lots of fun!

Famous fairytale siblings:

Hansel and Gretel –

The Three Little Pigs –

Cinderella and the STEP-sisters –

That wild bunch that lived in the shoe with their mother –

Jack and Jill (not confirmed, but likely siblings in the pattern of brothers who hastened the downfall of their siblings) –

My perfect sister who baked gold bars in her toy oven and made me very rich for life.

(That's STILL my fairytale!)

Stories Sisters Share

I've forgotten most of the details
of our childhood, but there is a
distinct impression of a little
madness and a lot of magic.

Once, we worked up the nerve
to sneak in with a flashlight
when our mother was taking a nap,
and oh-so-gently part her hair
to see if we could find the eyes
in the back of her head.
We didn't, but at the time we decided
they could have been closed.

One scorching Midwestern summer,
we got the neighborhood kids together
and tried to fry an egg on the sidewalk
because Mama said it was hot enough
to fry an egg on the sidewalk.

We couldn't understand why she didn't
appreciate that we were only following her
inspiration.

Early in life, our mother introduced us to the phrase "talk to him like a Dutch Uncle." We kids thought it meant to talk to someone, using great wisdom and kindness, in an over-exaggerated, sing-songy Dutch accent.

We'd use 'Dutch Uncle' talk on each other something like this:

"Ja, it voot bee goot eef you vould ahct joor age unt not joor shoe size!"

The content of the message wasn't nearly as therapeutic as the delivery, which cracked us up and pretty much put a stop to any bad behavior.

Try it... ;-)

Parents!
Stop the madness!
No more matching Easter outfits!

(As long as photos last.
your kids will never live it down!)

Long after we were grown, my sister revealed her strategy for avoiding punishment when we were kids.

She said she watched me be the stoic (fool), taking the punishment when we all got in trouble. When the parents got to her, she fell on the floor and started crying hysterically. Then our mother rushed to her rescue every time.

"Oh, poor child! It's alright, honey! There, there…"

The little faker never got in trouble!

I would like to formally recognize my siblings at this time for surviving, along with me, incredible childhood pranks.

Okay, who has cut a little bit of sister or brother's hair when they weren't looking and secretly relished it any time they yelled at you? Anyone? Anyone?

I really got into trouble for giving my sister a bar of soap and telling her it was white chocolate.

(But it was so worth it!)

Sometimes we spent long stretches of time cooped up in the house with nothing to do. That's what happened when we made cookies with little pieces of laxative that looked like chocolate chunks and served them to the kids next door.

Deacon told our parents he believed we were very close to God because there were so many prayers said for us. "God, please save us from those kids!"

I played pranks on my younger
siblings until the summer when
they suddenly outgrew me.
Their first act of revenge was
to spray whipped cream in my
face and then call the family dog
to give me a kiss. **Yuck!**

I loved to ruin Victorian
novels for my sister by offering
to read them to her. Just when
the hero was confessing his
undying love, I'd change the
romantic lines to words like
"pimple" and "stinky feet".

Sisters...

Growing up I declared her a human blister.
With others around,
I dismissed her and dissed her.
But now and again,
I just could have kissed her
Since we're on our own,
and I've desperately missed her –
My ally, my rival, my buddy...
my sister.

What Would Life be without Family?

FAMILY RECIPE:
One part adoration,
one part aggravation,
a heaping dose of patience,
and sarcasm on the side.

It's so easy,
while we're still young,
to take our family
for granted...

...but looking back,
we begin to understand
a little better the meaning
of home and the gift of
those we call family.

Why do reality shows bill themselves as "the biggest competition on the planet?" I'll show you the biggest competition on the planet. Come by our family reunion!

Modern families look like the UN today. Our family is African and Native American-Scandinavian-Latino-Chinese-Irish-French, and that doesn't include the spouses.

When we go out, we're a conversation piece, that's for sure. Oh, who am I kidding—we are a conversation convention.

We talk about a mother's glow
and praise her on a special day.
Books record what mother's know.
And even dad's "love and obey."

Yet, mud pies, clay, and finger paint
make any honest mom confess
the truth - this isn't for the faint:
Motherhood can be icky business.

Our family adopted a special holiday
greeting card that we've copied and
shared between our diverse clan:

Happy Merry Christmas-Hannuk-Kwanz-
Chinese New-Ramad-Cinco de Mayo-
Thanks-Labor-Independence Day!

Fond memories of home
and family are found
in the loving eyes
of my sister.

My siblings were such willing test subjects –
happy to eat pseudo-food cooked by a lightbulb
in a toy baking oven. It wasn't exactly
the beginning of a career as a top chef,
but we learned an important life lesson:
icing covers a multitude of sins.

We have one sister who is – well, special.
She names everything. She has names for
her household plants and trees in the yard,
and she's named every car she's ever owned.
The cars had biblical names for a long time:
Moses, Solomon, and Balthazar (affectionately
known as "Zar-car").

Then she moved into her virtuous auto phase,
and the next cars were Grace, Faith,
and the current – Hope.

Yeah, she's a little weird…in a whimsical,
wonderful sort of way.

There's something special about the sister of your parent. They slip you money and gum over the protests of your parents. They buy you cool clothes and presents that make your parents raise an eyebrow. And they tell you stories about growing up that a kid can hold over a parent like a get-out-of-jail card.

Yeah, they can be weird – there's always one with a hair growing out of a mole on her chin, and one that laughs too loudly, squeezes hard, and gives sloppy kisses.

But aunts are good for lifelong memories that'll make you smile just at the thought of them.

Everyone has relatives with bizarre nicknames. I had an Aunt Toe. Nobody could ever explain where that name came from, but it stuck like a corn pad.

Actually, it was Aunt Toe's sister, Ophelia who had the wacky toes. (Arthritis!) She wore one-size too small pumps with peek-a-boo cut out toes. She wrapped her poor aching toes with a mixture of liquid analgesic and cotton balls and then pulled her support hose over all of that. The net effect was a swollen, painful looking mass bulging out of the toe hole of her shoe.

She was amazingly pleasant.

Fatherhood is a man's chance
to transition from being just a
goofy guy to being a "cool dad"
who's goofy because he's
entertaining his kid.

Boy-children – they're the same at
any age: they just grow bigger –
they don't grow up!
Girls spend girlhood being grown
and adulthood in search
of the girl unknown.

My Grandma liked to quote the old adage, "the acorn doesn't fall far from the tree." Then she'd say our whole family is nuts, and gleefully proclaim Grandpa the head-nut-in-charge.

That made Grandpa throw his head back and laugh and laugh.

They're the official relationship role models for the kids in the family.

(The grownups, too.)

Grands –
both young and old –
are hopeless conspirators
and natural allies.

Behind the wheel of a car, my mild-mannered, super-professional dad turns into a kamikaze, daredevil, rollercoaster driving, maniacal cartoon-like character.

Riding with him has taught us prayer really works.

My friends look at me strangely when I tell them I was my daddy's "road dog" when I was little. They don't understand what a privilege it was for a little girl to ride with Dad to run errands on his day off.

Ah, the weekend… that time when virtual strangers sharing the same address all week come together for bonding and rivalry.

Then in a blink, it's Monday – the return to normalcy and the realization that family rocks and normal isn't nearly as much fun.

Mothers go though a point in life when they're perpetually hot, mad, and a little frantic...

But by then, their loved ones are totally devoted to them and willing to duck and disappear as needed, until Mom feels better.

Moms deserve a pass.

The Sister Rules

When relatives contact one sister
with creative gift ideas for the
other sister, the contacted sister
will firmly insist: just get her what
she asked for!

When one sister's sweetheart
asks the other sister how to
make amends, sister two will
excuse herself and sneak a call
to sister one for the answer.

There will be no tattling when
one sister invokes the failsafe
"cross your heart."

Under no circumstances will
a sister ever comment on
the other sister's weight gain.
Weight loss, however, is an
entirely different matter and
should always be noticed.

No one will say or infer that sister
is getting like Mom in any possible
way. (Unless of course she's into
that kind of thing.)

No sibling will trump a sister's
good news when it's either
a pregnancy, a marriage,
or a new job. Observe the
six-month window of humility.

If you like it, you may buy it in your size, but always check before you wear it to make certain your sister hadn't planned to wear it. (Or didn't just wear it with the same crowd last week!)

When one sister borrows it, she may play crazy and keep it as long as the other sister doesn't ask for it back. However, she must surrender it immediately and in ready condition upon request.

No sibling will side with a third party against a sister.

Likewise, no sibling will ever undermine a sister's parenting. Even if she used to do the same thing she's telling her kids never to do. Especially then.

The Sister Rules

A sister will bring a sick sister
chicken soup and flu remedies
even though she will expose
herself to the evil virus.

(This card to be used only when
there are no other willing players.)

No pushing buttons.
You know the ones.
The ones nobody else
even knows are there.

A good sister will not
mention her sister's moustache,
but will buy her sister a salon
hair removal gift certificate.

No one will talk, laugh,
or otherwise interrupt a
sister's favorite television
drama.

A good sister will not leave out one ingredient in a shared recipe, nor change the measurement just to be able to say hers always tastes better.

A sister will not stage a televised intervention if her sister becomes a hoarder and recluse who doesn't open the door to anyone, as long as the sister continues at least to open the door for her.

A sister has known since high school that she can call any time of the day or night, stranded anywhere, and her sister will come to the rescue.

A sister will always tell a sister
if there is a pimple on her nose,
her skirt tucked in her under-
wear, a curler in her hair,
vegetables in her teeth,
pantyhose trailing from one
pant leg, or garlic odor on
her fingers. And she will never
tell it so anyone else can hear.

If you like it so well that you think
you ought to keep it, your sister will
love it. Give it to her.

Sisters rule.

The Sisterhood Fallacies

You could risk a perfectly wonderful sister
relationship if you believe these things.

You don't need to apologize!
Time will smooth everything out.

Anytime your sister is on the
outs with mom, that's more
positive mom attention for
the other sister.

The last one to reach out after
a quarrel is the strongest.

Sisters will forgive you
if you forget their birthday.

Pointing out your sister's faults
in a constructive way will help
her succeed, and she'll thank you!

Walk a mile in your sister's shoes.
Go on! Dare you—especially the
brand-new, cute ones.
Without asking. Before she gets
to wear them.

Sisters have to have similar lifestyles, beliefs, and viewpoints in order to get along great.

Words don't matter, like "sticks and stones…"

THE TRUTH about sisters is… she who occasionally needs and gets confirmation, reassurance, and encouragement from a sister is to be envied.

Lucky girl.

Borrow. Take. Share.

Things Sisters Borrow...
Clothes, books, makeup, curling
irons, accessories, jewelry,
Hair doo-dads, laptops, you!

Things Sisters Take...
Clothes, accessories, photos,
recipes, boyfriends, time for you...
and when needed, they'll steal
you away!

Things Sisters Share...
Clothes – shoes – bedrooms –
bathrooms – secrets – ideas –
parents – experiences – recipes –
history – information (about teachers,
guys, friends, life), each other.

Sisters Borrow Sisters...

My sister used to borrow me to give her an excuse to go see animated movies that she really wanted to see. She didn't want "the crowd" to see her going into those movies at her age.

It was really cool for me, though, because I liked those kinds of movies, too, and my "crowd" got to see me hanging out with my big sister. Cool!

Sisters Heist!

She's a phenomenal mother! Wow! Your sister. But let's face it, she's been on relentless mommy duty for how many weeks since birth now? Her life has been constant feeding, burping, wiping, changing, washing, sleep...repeat.

It's time for a sister heist! Grab a cousin, best friend, (or good old Mom) to babysit for an afternoon, and steal your sister away for a massage, movie and tea and cookies. Can you find your old childhood tea set? Even better.

SISTERS TAKING SISTERS...

After so many years of marriage,
my sister and her husband are really close.
Their kids are all off being grownups and doing well.
They're finally at a place in life
when they can travel a bit and enjoy themselves.

I love how good my brother-in-law
has been to my sister,
but a little space is a good thing
for sweethearts now and then.

So we plan a sister day
like we used to have.
I pick her up early and we spend
a whole day together.

Her husband (what a guy!)
is always very happy and encouraging
when we leave, but waiting at the window
when we come back.

That's what I wished for her once upon a time.

When I travel. I can room with anyone.
I can get along with every kind of personality.
I shared a bedroom with a sister. Believe me,
over the course of time. it seemed she was
many different people.
(Especially when mom was around.)

I gave my sister permission to date
an old boyfriend one time. She said,
"thanks for the offer, but I didn't
want your hand-me-down shoes,
what makes you think I'd take your
left-over blues?"

SISTERS SHARE...

I signed up for one of those genome projects that tell you your history from a swab of the inside of your cheek. I shared the results with my sister and we were both blown away to think of the women in our family as survivors who faced adversity, conquered the wild, raised food and children, and traveled over continents to begin life as pioneers in a new country. It was a moving experience that we just had to share with our mother.

Mom said, "It doesn't surprise me at all that you girls discovered these inspiring things about our background. Of course, you know that's all about my side of the family. Fortunately, those extraordinary genes overcame the Neanderthals on your father's side."

If Bible Characters Had Sisters...

Cain would've had a sympathetic ear and may have been able to just talk it out.

John the Baptist would've at least had some chocolate-chip cookies to go with those locusts.

Methuselah would've heard about those dorky sandals for the next 954 years.

Job would've had even MORE "helpful advisers" in his business!

I don't care if there were already two random cats on the ark, Noah would've had to take Fluffy, and that's that.

Sisters Say: Proverbs For Our Sisters

A PROVERB SAYS?
"A child must creep
until it learns to walk."

SISTERS SAY:
The child with an older sister
gets a head start on learning
everything. No wonder she
often succeeds!

A PROVERB SAYS?
"A talkative child reveals
his parents' secrets."

SISTERS SAY:
Sister secrets are much
more fun to spill!

A PROVERB SAYS?
"Borrowed clothes do not keep one warm."

SISTERS SAY:
But they're sooooo much fun!!!!
It's totally worth it!

A PROVERB SAYS?
"You may change the clothes,
but you cannot change the man."

SISTERS SAY:
Seriously, what do men know about
clothes? Treat your sister to a fab
new outfit and just see how big of a
ripple that can make.

A PROVERB SAYS?
"Disclose not your defects
even to a friend."

SISTERS SAY:
That friend doesn't sound like much
fun. Luckily, sisters know our faults
and (mostly) love us anyway!

A PROVERB SAYS?
"That which does not kill us
makes us stronger."
- Nietzsche

SISTERS SAY:
Sometimes I think I owe my very
life and strength to my sister.

A PROVERB SAYS?
"Many hands make light work."(John Heywood)

SISTERS SAY:
Many hands can spoil the broth, like too many cooks.
(What does Mama always say? "Keep your hands to yourself.")

A PROVERB SAYS?
"Praise the child and
you praise the mother."

SISTERS SAY:
Praise the child and
you'd better praise
the sister, too.

A PROVERB SAYS?
"The wheel that squeaks the loudest
is the wheel that gets the grease." (Josh Billings)

SISTERS SAY:
Have you met my sister?
We call her "Slick."

A PROVERB SAYS?
"Having an only child
is like having one eye."

SISTERS SAY:
Yeah! We totally agree!

Sisters Dishing & Reminiscing

We tell our kids about the brand new experience of going to the first fast-food drive-thru to open in our neighborhood. The looks they give us! Now we know what it feels like to be a fossil in a museum.

Isn't it funny how many cool inventions we thought up over time, sis? Little squares of paper with glue on one end to make them stick...rocks that we gathered from the yard and painted messages on...round headed people with 2 round eyes and a smile... Imagine how rich we would be if... Oh, don't cry! We just have to keep thinking. We'll go for it next time.

For years we hated covering our
legs with pantyhose.
But now that pantyhose are
passé, our once-perfect legs could
use a little camouflage.

For the longest time, my sister
and I were hooked on the
daytime soaps. We'd call each
other and talk about the plots
as though they were happen-
ing to real people. Soap opera
characters are like imaginary
friends for grown-ups.

Everyone always said I took after my father's side of the family and my sister took after my mother's side of the family, but when you put us together, we looked related. That's somehow strange how that works out.

It's a bizarre thing watching someone who you once witnessed growing leg hair suddenly growing a human being in her belly.
It must be immortalized in pictures.

My sister and I have this sort of telepathy that is positively uncanny! Even though we're miles away, I'll call her up and say, "what did you fix for dinner?' and she'll say "chicken," and I'll say, "that's what I fixed!" And she'll say, "what did you fix with it?" And I'll say "potatoes, corn and salad," and she'll say, "that's what I fixed!" Of course, Dad will tell you whenever Mom made chicken she also fixed potatoes, corn and salad. Wow! What are the odds?!

The women in our family are very vain, we must admit. Our grandmother always wore her high-heeled shoes that matched her purse, and she had cotton handkerchiefs and gloves to match, and earring and necklaces. She'd swipe her berry lipstick on her little duck lips and pucker them together, clear into her 80's. Vanity, thy name is woman! There's nothing wrong with pretending you feel good until you can feel better. As a matter of fact, it actually helps.

It was the ultimate no-no! My brother-in-law-to-be asked me what he really needed to know about my sister. It was one of the only times in my life that I came close to dying. I thought I'd choke to death and pass out from the pain of biting my tongue.

It hardly seems possible that we predate microwaves, dishwashers, instant coffee, the internet, cell phones, and the original coffee shop chain. We prefer not to think of it as being old – just ahead of our time.

We studied the ankles of the older women in our family for years, noting how they were a little elephantine, with ankle backs cracked to rival the Sahara! It's just another instance of the many things girls can learn from their elders. We started moisturizing like our ankles depended on it long ago.

Ha, ha, ha! Remember how we used to laugh at the thought that we could end up with grandma's mouth and grandpa's teeth?

Kids, don't laugh about things like that. Pray – pray hard!

My sister and I had our childhood idols… at first, both of us were gaga over the same rock 'n' roll star. Then I became enamored with a star who was lead singer of a family band on television. She went bonkers over a handsome movie star with a baritone voice. Our room was a battle of the idol posters.

I'll see your movie star and raise you a singer who plays guitar.

My sister is a kind of label snob. She's always identified with her automobile as a sign of achievement. She calls her purses and shoes by their designer's names, and she talks about movie star gossip, calling them by their first names as if she knows them personally! I tend to think that the best indicators of superiority are the ones that show how much money I can save with perfectly good and functional stuff. She calls me a Neanderthal; I call her the great pretender and she calls me a commoner. We're crazy about each other. There's nothing like having someone in your life who totally gets you.

A Sister's Bill Of Rights

You have the right to remain silent when your sister asks if you think she looks like Mom.

You have the right to peacefully assemble a casserole without your sister butting in.

You have the right to free speech, but criticizing your sister's boyfriend is probably gonna cost you.

No self-incrimination. If you don't know where your sister's blouse got to all by itself, you don't have to answer any questions.

No unreasonable search and seizure. Did your sister forget to lock her diary and write it in unbreakable code? Totally reasonable, go for it!

No double jeopardy. This means if you forgave your sister, you can't bring that particular fight up in a new fight, no matter how solid your point.

Right to a speedy trial. If your sister seems to be sulking, she must spit out what exactly is eating her within three days or get over it. You too.

Eminent domain does not apply. If your shoes are on your sister's side of the room, or you left Mom's heirloom serving pieces at her house, she totally has to give them back.

No cruel and unusual punish-ment. Your sister totally cannot drag out the photos of you in seventh grade to show your new fiance.

Sweet Reflections

A Sister is the sweet reflection
of our family connection.

I used to look at my sister and
have mixed feelings of a little tinge
of jealousy and amazement
that she was so pretty.

My little sister used to look
at me with the strangest
expression…I couldn't figure
out if she admired me or
wanted me to fall on my
face. She was probably just
thinking about how funny
looking I was.

A sister is like a mirror,
reflecting back to you
the very best of who you are.

Our mom was fearless and creative when it came to child rearing. Once, my sister had a temper tantrum in a store, falling down screaming and kicking on the floor.

Mom just stared at her for a few seconds with a totally blank expression on her face and then she fell on the floor and started screaming and kicking, too.

After that, no one in our family had any more temper tantrums.

I thought my sister was so calm and laid back. It seemed nothing ever gets her upset. When things didn't go her way she just shrugged her shoulders and made a face like "oh well."

I gave her a hug for no reason every once in a while anyway.

I don't know why I always held everything inside like nothing ever bothered me. I did it so long that I felt like that's what everyone expected. I think people thought my feelings couldn't be hurt. Then my sister would just hug me out of the blue.

I thought she must be psychic.

When I had my first baby, I was woefully naive about everything. I'd seen too many pictures of blissed-out mothers rocking their equally blissed-out babies peacefully, without a care. My sister is the one who took me to Baby Boot Camp. After all, she'd done it all before. She patiently filled me in on everything from breastfeeding to colic to teething. The best thing is she had faith in me and kept assuring me I was doing great. Now all I want to know is, where was this helpfulness and patience when we were in junior high?

Dogs have the right idea —
there's no such thing as only
children in their world.
There's wrestling, tumbling,
and jockeying for position,
but there's always, always,
a kindred spirit right beside
them, ready to play.
That's how it should be.

I'll put my sister up against
any Bible woman. She's got
the supportiveness of Ruth,
the wisdom of Deborah,
the courage of Esther, the
faithfulness of Hannah...
oh, and the competitiveness
of Martha!

I'll tell you what to expect when you're expecting. Your sister to scare you with endless labor and delivery gross-out stories, then laugh. OK, since she's so much older and more experienced, guess who's probably going to have her gall bladder or some whatchamacallit out first when we're old. Right. And guess who's going to "volunteer" a pile of stories about some "friend" who could never eat dessert again, gained 150 pounds, and had to start wearing support hose. Me.

Sisters in Victorian novels are always smiling sweetly at each other while sitting around the fire doing needle-work. I don't buy it. They all had to huddle by the fire because their houses leaked like sieves and that was the only source of heat. And there was no TV, so they had to talk to each other or die of boredom. And you can bet there was competition over whose needlework was daintier. I bet half the time they were embroidering "Not even Charles Dickens thinks you're cute" in their little hoops.

My sister's the only one who knows when I exaggerate my background or abilities. But she lets me get away with it. She knows why I'm too insecure to be myself sometimes. But then I look at her, and realize she came from the same background, and she turned out to be a capable, confident woman - the things I pretend to be. So maybe, really... I am those things, too.

I try to remember my younger sister is all grown up, but I will always see her as in her early 20's, just starting out in life and in great need of my advice. With modern technology, though, it's easier for her to humor me. She can delete my emails without reading them, for all I know, and just write back "Thanks!"

It was rough growing up as the "little sister." Coming behind the older one, always painted with the same brush, no matter what – good or bad. Teachers who call you "little…" followed by your sister's name. Guys who give you a strange look that you don't know how to read when they find out you're so-and-so's little sister.

But there comes a day of liberation when a little sister manages to somehow side-step her sister's path and wind up with a bunch that knows nothing about the older sister. Then they become her sisters, too.

Sometimes it's hard being the older sister. My younger sister came along with so much more nuvo-techno savvy and exposure. I feel like a diesel station wagon in a world of hybrids. When she outdoes me at something, though, I tell myself that of course, she had my wisdom and example to give her a big boost. That way I get to take credit and not feel jealous. After all, I'm a classic!

I look at my sister's profile on her social network page and think, "Do I even know this woman? Since when did she kayak?" But I realize that's how she wants to be seen by the world. I guess she can't trust all outsiders to accept her for who she is. But she already knows I accept and love her for who she is. I don't snark about her little fabricated life, but I'm going to think of something special for us to do that isn't "fabulous" at all. Maybe sharing some of Grandma's old cookie recipes.

Sisters...

Spicy, Sweet, and Sour.

Sisters are like glazed doughnuts...
they'll draw you in with their
warmth and sweetness and then
bend you all out of shape.

A sister is someone
who knew you
as a bratty,
snot-nosed kid...
and never fails
to remind you of it.

Mozart had a sister, but she
never achieved the fame he
did because she was probably
busy cleaning and cooking.
What's my sister's excuse?

Of course,
Shakespeare had a sister.
Where do you think he
learned all those insults?

I wonder what it's like to be the
plainer sister of a legendary beauty.
I'll have to ask my sister.

My sister's children turned
out surprisingly cool. I wish I
could take credit. But mostly
I remember goofing around to
make them laugh. It was my
sister who made them do
homework and taught them
good manners. Great, now I
have to stop teasing my sister
for being such a goody-goody.
It sure paid off.

Just because your sister doesn't
understand your lifestyle, approve
of your decisions, or think you can
sing karaoke worth a flip, doesn't
mean she doesn't love you.
Just because she doesn't think
your mangy dog is cute or your
husband is good enough for you
doesn't mean she won't step in
to help take care of either one
of them when there's a need.

And just because she thinks
your mom is a little bananas...
wait a minute, that's actually a
good bonding experience.

The seven sins of sisterhood…
- borrowing without asking
- listening without sympathizing
- online "status updates" without really communicating
- fishing for compliments without reciprocating
- criticizing without sugarcoating (just a little!)
- "forgiving" without forgetting
- desserts without sharing

My sister once gave me
the silent treatment
by refusing to write in her diary.

What guys can do
to each other with
roughhouse and
wrestling, sisters can
do with THE LOOK.

No one can top me
and my sister for
passive-aggressive notes.
During our pretentious
black turtleneck days
I left her a note in haiku form:

"Someone left a mess.
Dishes will not clean themselves.
Thanks, Your Loving Sis."

So she left me one back:

"You're bad at haiku.
Even worse at being cool.
I give it a D."

Luckily, neither of us actually
majored in writing.

Nobody cares that you were
a braces-wearing, knock-
kneed nerd in junior high.
Except your sister.
She'll never let you forget it.

The point of dating is to test
compatibility. I think it's a
fine tradition that needs to
be brought back. And while
we're at it, can we extend it
to sisters? Make sure you can
get along for the long haul
before you're stuck on some
surprise camping and hiking
vacation with a "Field Guide
to Edible Greens" and her
kissy-face, fru fru dog in a
backpack.

My sister decided to go on an all natural health food craze. She never thinks it's nearly as funny as the rest of the family on our get togethers when everyone else has a full plate of carbs, red meat and sugar, and then I put a bowl of dried oats and grass clippings in front of her. That one never gets old.

My sister is one of those rare perfect people who never does or says anything wrong. In that way, we're very much alike.

My sister carries a tote that says, "my other bag is my sister." Cute. I got her back. I made a bumper sticker for her car that says, "Rage is when your fat foot won't fit your sister's slipper."

Sisters enjoy the perfect balance of a lasting relationship – the embarrassing photos that keep each other in check.

I don't have to diet…
I just have to stay one
size smaller than my
sister at all times.
Then I'm satisfied.

Mother said she had the
two of us close together
so we'd have each other.
I used to think she meant
"…for friendship and
support." Nuh-uh. She
meant "…to help you both
learn patience."

Tolstoy: "Let us forgive each other—
then only will we live in peace."

My Sister and I: "Nanny Nanny, boo boo,
I'm telling! I'm telling!"

I think the most hilarious
fight my sister and I ever
had was over whose
hippie idol's peace songs
were most sincere and
meaningful. Yeah, it was
before the age of irony.

Girls have this universal word, "mean." It hardly ever refers to physical violence or even overt insult. It mostly implies not being loyal. "Mean girls" is universal shorthand for girls that gang up on another girl for sport. Sisters can be plenty annoying, plenty selfish, and plenty stuck-up, but hardly ever mete out the kind of betrayal that truly rises to the level of "mean." If you tell your sister some girls at school are being "mean," she'll instantly sympathize, and take their meanness personally. And hopefully, give them what for.

Life may not be a dress
rehearsal, but my sister
and I sure rehearsed some
comedy and drama. "Loafers
are for losers!" "Please!
No more velour pantsuits!"
We both should have
gotten Tony awards for
our haughty act.

The best inheritance a parent can give a child is a friend to share life's journey. Thanks a lot Mom, although $700,000 could have been a really fun lifelong friend!

If you get the flu, your sister will be there to bring you macaroni and cheese and old movies. If you get laid off, your sister will be there to soothe your ego and encourage you to keep positive. And one of these days, I'm going to treat her to a movie.

Sister Therapy:
Two spoons and a
half a gallon of ice cream.

"Laissez-faire" was invented by politicians to mean "hands off." Sisters don't need a fancy French word. They just need "THE LOOK."

My sister thinks she's Lady Annabelle, Baroness of the Hearth. But that's OK, I'm Lady Bringdown, Baroness of the Smart but Devastating Retort.

These days, it takes a technological genius to actually stop speaking to someone. You have to know how to purge them from social network sites, phones, blogs, GPS, picture tagging, and who knows what else? It's easier just to forget what happened and keep officially talking to your sister.

Why do they call it
"one-upmanship?"
My sister and I can
out-one-up any man,
anytime.

My sister knows the real me.
All my other friends believe the
wildly exaggerated stuff I post
on my social network page.

Just because your sister's advice turns out to be right doesn't mean your ego is ready to accept it. You can thank her when you're 80 and the only thing you have left to compete about is the crossword puzzle at the nursing home. She'll either understand or she'll have forgotten the whole thing.

If you ask me, there should be purple hearts for sisters who go out on a limb and apologize first. That's as much an act of courage as anything.

There are times when I just show up at my sister's door and she knows. We don't have to say a word. She points to the couch, tosses me a pillow, puts on the teapot, grabs a DVD and in a couple of hours all's right with the world.

When my first real relationship went down in flames, my sister kept the chocolate malts coming. She brought me piles of magazines and movies, and hid the phone and the computer. I'll always be grateful, but I don't know if I'll ever want another chocolate malt.

Lots of people say the cure for sadness is to face it one day at a time. I'm here to tell you the cure is to go running to your sister and cower under the covers, whining pitifully. Who doesn't see that?

I don't know much about quantum theory, but I know there's a force field around my sister that nobody better cross. Or I'll turn them into sub-ionized particles. If that's a thing.

Some people think the cure to a breakup is exercise. Others swear by new hairstyles, new wardrobes, exotic vacations, or (my least favorite) "getting back out there." Go ahead and give these a try — but if you ask me, there's nothing like a cool and understanding sister. Especially one who dishes on all her guy's annoying habits in hilarious detail, helping you realize that being coupled isn't always wonderful. What is always wonderful is having someone who cares about you, and knowing your sister always will.

LOVE is the foundation that smooths over
flaws and makes sisterhood beautiful.

EMPATHY is the mascara that runs
when she cries because you're hurt.

SUPPORT is the lipstick that puts a good face
on things and brightens any situation.

UNDERSTANDING is the concealer
that helps guard your secrets.

And PATIENCE is the hairspray
that gunks up the curling iron
when you're both in a hurry
and have to share.

Makeup analogies for great family ties!

I switched majors three times.
I didn't switch sisters once.
I think I knew a good thing
when I had it.

One good thing about getting
older is that sisters finally
mature out of competition,
judgment, sarcasm, and all
that. You get about three
good years together before
senility sets in.

I remember all the times I
collaborated with my sister
on the perfect outfit: How
does this look with this?
These shoes or those?
Try that top? Perfect! I Love it!
It's a wonder I ever get
dressed without her now.

You know that stage
we went through with
the matching outfits?
Suppose we'll revert
back to that in the
nursing home?
It'll be OK then.

Sisters bring comedy and
drama to your life's story…
and sometimes hankies
and brownies.

SISTERS:
Our traditions
are like the sweet fruit
that fills the middle of a pie —
holding the crusts together,
bringing us back again and again
with a big spoon.

The road from sister-
hood to friendship has
a lot of potholes on the
way. But, fortunately,
a lot of bakeries, ice
cream parlors, and cute
accessory shops too.

I remember asking my mom if we
could get a dog – a loyal friend
who'd play with me, tear up my
stuff, and be really happy when
I come around with food. She
brought home a sister instead.
Pretty much the same thing.

Moving from sisters to
friends is one step forward,
two steps back, and a lot of
steps on eggshells.
But it's worth it.

There are sisters by blessing
and there are sisters by birth.
The first develop over years of
caring, the second are there
through a lifetime of sharing.

Whether we admit it or not,
we all want our sisters to be proud of us.
That's most of why we get on the competition carousel.
If we didn't care, we wouldn't try so hard
to impress each other.

Do you have a pushy sister?
The type who's always in your
business, wanting to know
if you got ripped off, paid too
much, called the cable company
and gave them what for, or
took that blouse back and got a
refund? Keep on her good side.
That's who'll really be there
when your basement floods or
the insurance company keeps
stalling on reimbursing you.
Pushy people know how to
get stuff done and are in their
element when the chips are
down. At a time like that,
they're not annoying at all.

Partner in crime,
arch-enemy,
confidante,
blackmailer –
sisters are life's
walking contradiction.

Sisters can drive you crazy.
But then they turn around
and drive you to your
biopsy. And hold your
hand while you wait for
the results.

We developed a love for
shopping side by side,
flipping page by page
through the BIG Christmas
Toy catalog, turning back
the corners on the pages
with our faves, dreaming.

Let's never stop dreaming
and turning back the corners
on sweet memories – OK?

They're obvious twins— sisters who've
spent many a year in each other's company.
They appear to be in their 70's, but they're
actually 88. Their wispy gray hair swirling
around their heads like crowns still boasts
defiant strands of coal black.

To look at them, you just know exactly how
they looked at age two — just as you could
have seen them now to look at them as tod-
dlers. They are "characters" in every sense
of the word. They laugh with their mouths
gaped open, reaching out and patting each
other as they talk. Stories tumble from the
both of them in a jumble, phrases flowing
from one and then the other forming full
sentences punctuated with some words
said in unison now and then. They speak
with such excitement that they squeal; their
carefree is contagious. Without a conscious
thought, you'll find yourself smiling to watch
them, no tension — just wonder, like the first
time you saw butterflies.

That's the way to be sisters.
That's the way to be.

Accolades, awards, and acclaim
from people of great stature
can't compare to the approval
of someone who knew you as
a kid — hair streaming wild in
the wind, squealing with joy,
and smelling like big fun in the
summer sun.

If I could have chosen,
I would have picked an
entirely different sister.

It would have been one of
those rare occasions when
I would have been wrong.

My sister and I didn't say
"love ya" very often.
But we said "Be careful" a lot—
and it meant that and so much
more. Sometimes it meant "Don't
swing so high" or "Don't pedal so
fast." Later, it meant "Don't go to
that party" or "Don't trust that
guy." Still later it meant "Don't
take any risks 'till that baby's here
safe and sound." Now we're back
to where it means "Don't fall and
break a hip." But it always means,
"I'm looking out for you—
that's what I do."

The LORD bless thee, and keep thee:
Numbers 6:24